AUDIO ACCESS INCLUDED
Recorded Piano Accompaniments Online

AARON COPLAND

Old American Songs
for Clarinet and Piano

To access companion recorded piano accompaniments online, visit:
www.halleonard.com/mylibrary

Enter Code
8122-3045-3082-9567

BOOSEY & HAWKES

AN IMAGEM COMPANY

DISTRIBUTED BY

HAL•LEONARD®
CORPORATION
7777 W. BLUEMOUND RD. P.O. BOX 13819 MILWAUKEE, WI 53213

www.boosey.com
www.halleonard.com

The piano parts in this edition are the same as Copland's originals for voice and piano, but often transposed to a key suitable to the featured solo instrument. The solo instrumental part is a transcription of the vocal line of the originals, idiomatically adapted and arranged for the solo instrument. Articulations, ornaments and slightly varied melodies in spots make the songs more characteristic of instrumental solos.

Contents

FIRST SET

9   The Boatmen's Dance

14   The Dodger

20   Long Time Ago

23   Simple Gifts

26   I Bought Me a Cat

SECOND SET

33   The Little Horses

36   Zion's Walls

41   The Golden Willow Tree

48   At the River

51   Ching-a-ring Chaw

Pianist on the Recordings: Laura Ward

The price of this publication includes access to companion recorded piano accompaniments online,
for download or streaming, using the unique code found on the title page.
Visit **www.halleonard.com/mylibrary** and enter the access code.

Old American Songs is also available for Flute, Horn, Trumpet, Trombone, Violin and Cello.

Preface

The first set of *Old American Songs* was completed in 1950, the same year that Copland finished another major song set, *Twelve Poems of Emily Dickinson*. While Copland was composing the folksong settings, tenor Peter Pears and composer Benjamin Britten came to visit him. By this time Britten had composed many folksong settings himself as recital material for the performing duo of Pears and Britten (on piano). Taken by the new creative and inventive settings, they left with Copland's promise to send them copies of the songs to be performed in England. On October 17, 1950, the first set was given its world premiere by Pears and Britten at their Aldeburgh Festival. The American premiere took place in New York on January 28, 1951, with Copland accompanying baritone William Warfield.

The success of the first set prompted Copland to compose five more American song settings. Finished in 1952, the second set was premiered by Warfield and Copland at the Castle Hill Concerts in Massachusetts on July 24 of that year. Copland would later orchestrate both sets for medium voice and small orchestra. Warfield sang the premiere of the orchestrated first set with the Los Angeles Philharmonic, conducted by Alfred Wallenstein, on January 7, 1955. Mezzo-soprano Grace Bumbry premiered the orchestrated second set with the Ojai Festival Orchestra on May 25, 1955, with Copland on the podium as conductor.

FIRST SET
Song Origins, Copland Sources and Texts

The Boatmen's Dance (Minstrel Song – 1843)

Published in Boston in 1843 as an "original banjo melody" by Old Dan. D. Emmett, who later composed "Dixie." Source from the Harris Collection of American Poetry and Plays at Brown University.

Refrain:
High row the boatmen row,
floatin' down the river, the Ohio.
(the refrain repeats the two lines above)

The boatmen dance, the boatmen sing,
the boatmen up to ev'rything
And when the boatmen gets on shore
he spends his cash and works for more
Then dance the boatmen dance,
O dance the boatmen dance
O dance all night 'til the broad daylight
And go home with the gals in the mornin'.

Refrain

I went on board the other day
to see what the boatmen had to say
There I let my passion loose,
an' they cram me in the calaboose
Then dance the boatmen dance,
O dance the boatmen dance
O dance all night 'til the broad daylight
And go home with the gals in the mornin'.

Refrain

The boatman is a thrifty man
There's none can do as the boatman can
I never see a pretty gal in my life
But that she was a boatman's wife
Then dance the boatmen dance,
O dance the boatmen dance
O dance all night 'til the broad daylight
And go home with the gals in the mornin'.

Refrain

The Dodger (Campaign Song)

As sung by Mrs. Emma Dusenberry of Mena, Arkansas, who learned it in the 1880s. Supposedly used in the Cleveland-Blaine presidential campaign. Published by John A. and Alan Lomax in *Our Singing Country*.

Yes the candidate's a dodger, yes a well known dodger,
Yes the candidate's a dodger, yes and I'm a dodger too
He'll meet you and treat you and ask you for your vote
But look out boys he's a dodgin' for a note

Refrain:
Yes we're all dodgin', a-dodgin', dodgin', dodgin'
Yes we're all dodgin' out a way through the world.

Yes the preacher he's a dodger yes a well known dodger
Yes the preacher he's a dodger yes and I'm a dodger too
He'll preach you a gospel and tell you of your crimes
But look out boys he's a dodgin' for your dimes

Refrain

Yes the lover he's a dodger, yes a well known dodger
Yes the lover he's a dodger, yes and I'm a dodger too
He'll hug you and kiss you and call you his bride
But look out girls he's a tellin' you a lie

Refrain

Long Time Ago (Ballad)

Issued in 1837 by George Pope Morris, who adapted the words, and Charles Edward Horn, who arranged the music from an anonymous, original minstrel tune. Source from the Harris Collection at Brown University.

On the lake where droop'd the willow
Long time ago
Where the rock threw back the billow
Brighter than snow.

Dwelt a maid beloved and cherish'd
By high and low
But the autumn leaf she perish'd
Long time ago.

Rock and tree and flowing water
Long time ago
Bird and bee and blossom taught her
Love's spell to know

While to my fond words she listen'd
Murmuring low
Tenderly her blue eyes glisten'd
Long time ago.

Simple Gifts (Shaker Song)

A favorite song of the Shaker sect, from the period 1837–47. The melody and words were quoted by Edward D. Andrews in his book of Shaker rituals, songs and dances, entitled *The Gift to Be Simple*.

'Tis the gift to be simple 'tis the gift to be free
'Tis the gift to come down where you ought to be
And when we find ourselves in the place just right
'Twill be in the valley of love and delight.
When true simplicity is gained
To bow and to bend we shan't be ashamed
To turn, turn will be our delight
'Till by turning, turning we come round right.

I Bought Me a Cat (Children's Song)

A children's nonsense song. This version was sung to the composer by the American playwright Lynn Riggs, who learned it during his boyhood in Oklahoma.

I bought me a cat
My cat pleased me
I fed my cat under yonder tree
My cat says fiddle eye fee

I bought me a duck
My duck pleased me
I fed my duck under yonder tree
My duck says "Quaa, quaa"
My cat says fiddle eye fee

I bought me a goose
My goose pleased me
I fed my goose under yonder tree
My goose says "Quaw, quaw"
My duck says "Quaa, quaa"
My cat says fiddle eye fee

I bought me a hen
My hen pleased me
I fed my hen under yonder tree
My hen says "Shimmy shack, shimmy shack"
My goose says "Quaw, quaw"
My duck says "Quaa, quaa"
My cat says fiddle eye fee

I bought me a pig
My pig pleased me
I fed my pig under yonder tree
My pig says "Griffey, griffey"
My hen says "Shimmy shack, shimmy shack"
etc. (all the previous animals)

I bought me a cow
My cow pleased me
I fed my cow under yonder tree
My cow says "Baw, baw"
My pig says "Griffey, griffey"
etc.

I bought me a horse
My horse pleased me
I fed my horse under yonder tree
My horse says "Neigh, neigh"
My cow says "Baw, baw"
etc.

I bought me a wife
My wife pleased me
I fed my wife under yonder tree
My wife says "Honey, honey"
My horse says "Neigh, neigh"
etc.

SECOND SET
Song Origins and Copland's Sources

The Little Horses (Lullaby)
A children's lullaby song originating in the southern states, date
unknown. This adaptation was founded in part on John A. and
Alan Lomax's version published in *Folk Song U.S.A.*

Hush you bye,
Don't you cry,
Go to sleepy little baby.
When you wake,
You shall have,
All the pretty little horses.

Blacks and bays,
Dapples and grays,
Coach and six-a little horses.
(repeat the three lines above)

Hush you bye,
Don't you cry,
Go to sleepy little baby.
When you wake,
You'll have sweet cake, and
All the pretty little horses.

A brown and a gray
and a black and a bay and a
Coach and six-a little horses.
(repeat the three lines above)

Hush you bye,
Don't you cry,
Oh you pretty little baby.
Go to sleepy little baby.
Oh you pretty little baby.

Zion's Walls (Revivalist Song)
Original melody and words credited to John G. McCurry,
compiler of the Social Harp. Published by George P. Jackson in
Down East Spirituals.

Come fathers and mothers
Come sisters and brothers come,
Come join us in singing the praises of Zion,
the praises of Zion.

O fathers don't you feel determined
to meet within the walls of Zion,
We'll shout and go round,
We'll shout and go round,
We'll shout and go round,
We'll shout and go round the walls of Zion,
the walls of Zion.

Come fathers and mothers
Come sisters and brothers come,
Come join us in singing the praises of Zion.

Come fathers and mothers
Come sisters and brothers come,
Come join us in singing the praises of Zion,

O fathers don't you feel determined
to meet within the walls of Zion,
We'll shout and go round,
We'll shout and go round,
We'll shout and go round,
We'll shout and go round the walls of Zion,
the walls of Zion.

The Golden Willow Tree (Anglo-American Ballad)
Variant of the well-known Anglo-American ballad, more usually
called "The Golden Vanity." This version is based on a recording
issued by the Library of Congress Music Division from its
collection of the Archive of American Folk Song. Justus Begley
recorded it with banjo accompaniment for Alan and Elizabeth
Lomax in 1937.

There was a little ship in South Amerikee,
Crying O the land that lies so low,
There was a little ship in South Amerikee,
She went by the name of the Golden Willow Tree,
As she sailed in the lowland lonesome low,
As she sailed in the lowland so low.

We hadn't been a-sailin' more than two weeks or three,
Till we came in sight of the British Roverie,
As she sailed in the lowland lonesome low,
As she sailed in the lowland so low.

Up stepped a little carpenter boy
Says "What will you give me for the ship that I'll destroy?"
"I'll give you gold or I'll give thee,
I'll give you gold or I'll give thee,
the fairest of my daughters as she sails upon the sea,
If you'll sink 'em in the lowland lonesome low,
If you'll sink 'em in the land that lies so low."

[Note: the following section of Copland's setting
was cut in the solo instrumental adaptation.]

He turned upon his back and away swum he,
He swum till he came to the British Roverie,
He had a little instrument fitted for his use,
He bored nine holes and he bored them all at once.
He turned upon his breast and back swum he,
He swum till he came to the Golden Willow Tree,
"Captain, O Captain, come take me on board,
O Captain, O Captain, come take me on board,
And do unto me as good as your word
For I sank 'em in the lowland lonesome low,
I sank 'em in the lowland so low.

Oh no I won't take you on board,
Oh no, I won't take you on board,
Nor do unto you as good as my word,
Though you sank 'em in the lowland lonesome low,
Though you sank 'em in the land that lies so low."

"If it wasn't for the love that I have for your men,
I'd do unto you as I done unto them,
I'd sink you in the lowland lonesome low,
I'd sink you in the lowland so low."

He turned upon his head and down swum he,
He turned upon his head and down swum he,
He swum till he came to the bottom of the sea.
Sank himself in the lowland lonesome low,
Sank himself in the land that lies so low.

At the River (Hymn Tune)
Words and melody are by Rev. Robert Lowry, 1865.

Shall we gather by the river,
Where bright angels feet have trod,
With its crystal tide forever
Flowing by the throne of God.

Yes we'll gather by the river,
The beautiful, the beautiful river,
Gather with the saints by the river
That flows by the throne of God.

Soon we'll reach the shining river,
Soon our pilgrimage will cease,
Soon our happy hearts will quiver
With the melody of peace.

Yes we'll gather by the river,
The beautiful, the beautiful river,
Gather with the saints by the river
That flows by the throne of God.

Ching-a-ring Chaw (Minstrel Song)
The words have been adapted from the original, in the Harris Collection of American Poetry and Plays at Brown University.

Ching-a-ring-a ring ching ching,
Ho-a ding-a ding kum larkee,
Ching-a-ring-a ring ching ching,
Ho-a ding-a ding kum larkee.

Brothers gather round,
Listen to this story,
'Bout the promised land,
An' the promised glory.

You don' need to fear,
If you have no money,
You don' need none there,
To buy you milk and honey.

There you'll ride in style,
Coach with four white horses,
There the evenin' meal,
Has one two three four courses.

Ching-a-ring-a ring ching ching,
Ho-a ding-a ding kum larkee,
Ching-a-ring-a ring ching ching,
Ho-a ding-a ding kum larkee.

Nights we all will dance,
To the harp and fiddle,
Waltz and jig and prance,
"Cast off down the middle."

When the mornin' come,
All in grand and splendor,
Stand out in the sun,
And hear the holy thunder.

Brothers hear me out,
The promised land's a-comin',
Dance and sing and shout,
I hear them harps a-strummin'.

Ching-a-ring ching ching,
ching-a-ring ching ching,
Ching-a-ching ching-a-ching,
ching-a-ching ching-a-ching,
Ching-a-ring ching ching,
Ching-a-ring ching ching,
Ching-a ring-a ching-a ring-a
ching-a ring-a
Ring ching ching ching Chaw.

HIRSCHFELD 60

THE BOATMEN'S DANCE
(Minstrel Song-1843)

Arranged by AARON COPLAND
Adapted and arranged for clarinet by Bryan Stanley

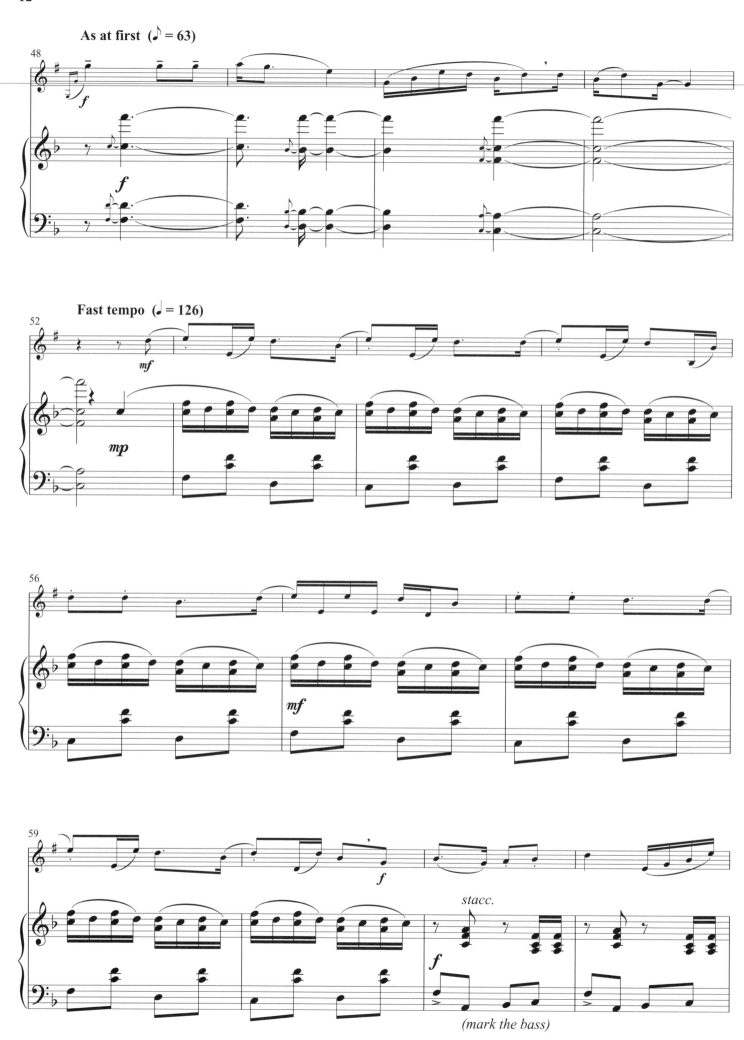

THE DODGER
(Campaign Song)

Arranged by AARON COPLAND
Adapted and arranged for clarinet by Bryan Stanley

LONG TIME AGO
(Ballad)

Arranged by AARON COPLAND
Adapted and arranged for clarinet by Bryan Stanley

Ped.   ✳

SIMPLE GIFTS
(Shaker Song)

Arranged by AARON COPLAND
Adapted and arranged for clarinet by Bryan Stanley

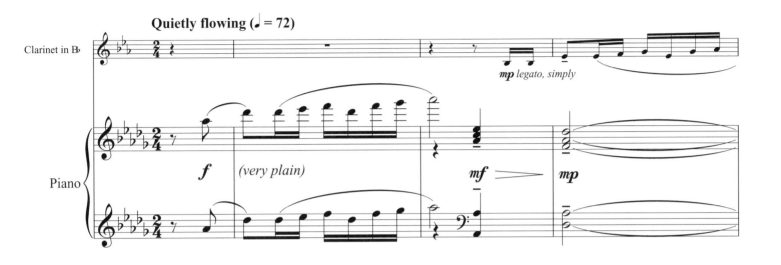

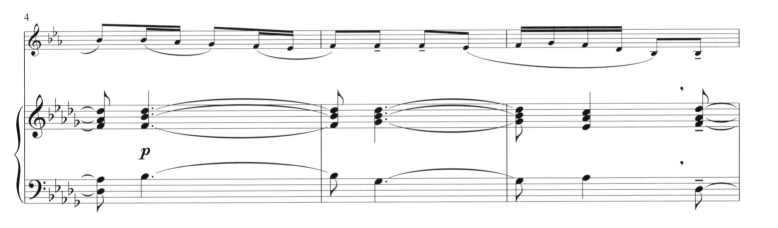

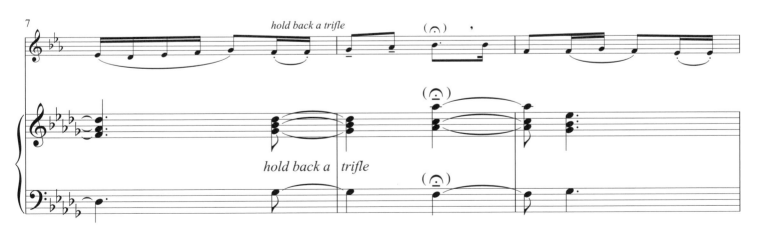

24

I BOUGHT ME A CAT
(Children's Song)

Arranged by AARON COPLAND
Adapted and arranged for clarinet by Bryan Stanley

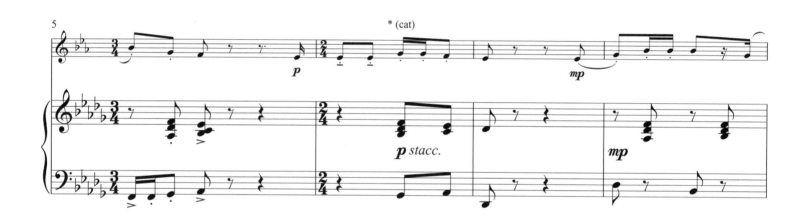

* The lyrics describe several animal sounds as well as the voice of a wife. We have indicated these as a reference for the instrumental performer.

AUDIO ACCESS INCLUDED
Recorded Piano Accompaniments Online

CLARINET

AARON COPLAND

Old American Songs
for Clarinet and Piano

Contents

FIRST SET

2   The Boatmen's Dance

4   The Dodger

6   Long Time Ago

7   Simple Gifts

8   I Bought Me a Cat

SECOND SET

10   The Little Horses

12   Zion's Walls

14   The Golden Willow Tree

17   At the River

18   Ching-a-ring Chaw

The solo instrumental part is a transcription of the vocal line of the originals, idiomatically adapted and arranged for the solo instrument. Articulations, ornaments and slightly varied melodies in spots make the songs more characteristic of instrumental solos.

To access companion recorded piano accompaniments online, visit:
www.halleonard.com/mylibrary

Enter Code
4716-4017-6712-3439

BOOSEY & HAWKES

AN IMAGEM COMPANY

DISTRIBUTED BY

HAL•LEONARD®
CORPORATION

7777 W. BLUEMOUND RD. P.O. BOX 13819 MILWAUKEE, WI 53213

www.boosey.com
www.halleonard.com

THE BOATMEN'S DANCE
(Minstrel Song-1843)

Clarinet in B♭

Arranged by AARON COPLAND
Adapted and arranged for clarinet by Bryan Stanley

THE DODGER
(Campaign Song)

Clarinet in B♭

Arranged by AARON COPLAND
Adapted and arranged for clarinet by Bryan Stanley

LONG TIME AGO
(Ballad)

Clarinet in B♭

Arranged by AARON COPLAND
Adapted and arranged for clarinet by Bryan Stanley

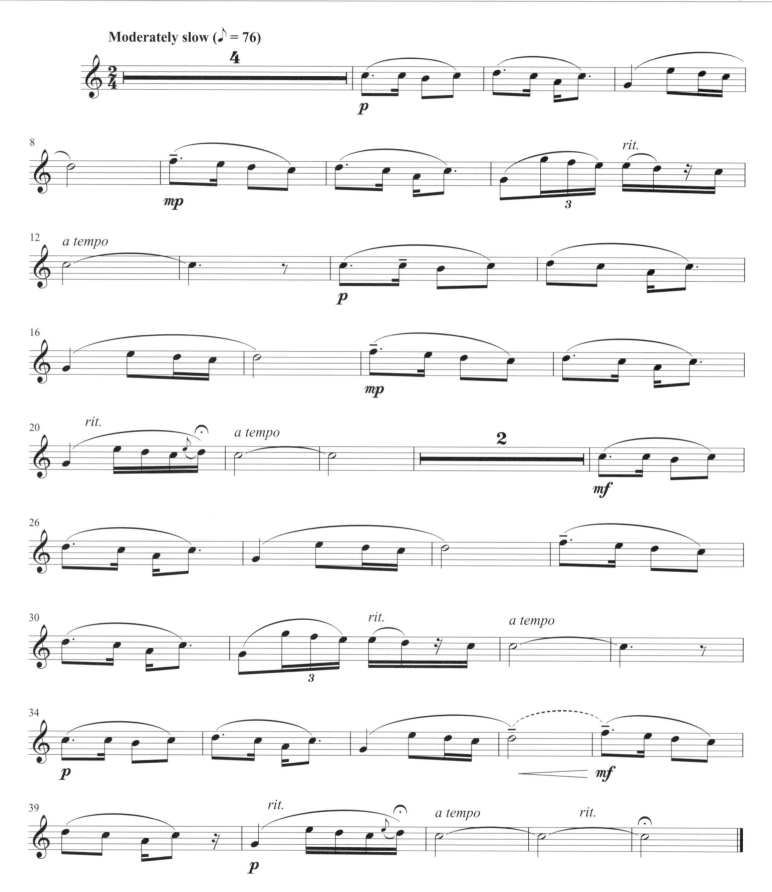

SIMPLE GIFTS
(Shaker Song)

Arranged by AARON COPLAND
Adapted and arranged for clarinet by Bryan Stanley

Clarinet in B♭

I BOUGHT ME A CAT
(Children's Song)

Clarinet in B♭

Arranged by AARON COPLAND
Adapted and arranged for clarinet by Bryan Stanley

* The lyrics describe several animal sounds as well as the voice of a wife. We have indicated these as a reference for the instrumental performer.

THE LITTLE HORSES
(Lullaby)

Arranged by AARON COPLAND
Adapted and arranged for clarinet by Bryan Stanley

Clarinet in B♭

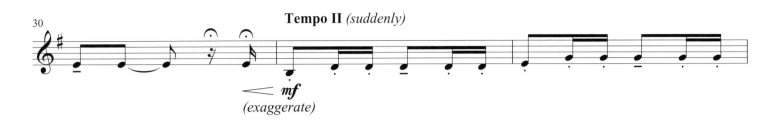

Tempo II *(suddenly)*

As at first *(slowly)*

ZION'S WALLS
(Revivalist Song)

Clarinet in B♭

Arranged by AARON COPLAND
Adapted and arranged for clarinet by Bryan Stanley

THE GOLDEN WILLOW TREE
(Anglo-American Ballad)

Clarinet in B♭

Arranged by AARON COPLAND
Adapted and arranged for clarinet by Bryan Stanley

Note: "The Golden Willow Tree" has been abbreviated with a cut due to its length of strophic verses in Copland's original.

HIRSCHFELD 60

AT THE RIVER
(Hymn Tune)

Arranged by AARON COPLAND
Adapted and arranged for clarinet by Bryan Stanley

Clarinet in B♭

CHING-A-RING CHAW
(Minstrel Song)

Clarinet in B♭

Arranged by AARON COPLAND
Adapted and arranged for clarinet by Bryan Stanley

THE LITTLE HORSES
(Lullaby)

Arranged by AARON COPLAND
Adapted and arranged for clarinet by Bryan Stanley

ZION'S WALLS
(Revivalist Song)

Arranged by AARON COPLAND
Adapted and arranged for clarinet by Bryan Stanley

THE GOLDEN WILLOW TREE
(Anglo-American Ballad)

Arranged by AARON COPLAND
Adapted and arranged for clarinet by Bryan Stanley

Note: "The Golden Willow Tree" has been abbreviated with a cut due to its length of strophic verses in Copland's original.

AT THE RIVER
(Hymn Tune)

Arranged by AARON COPLAND
Adapted and arranged for clarinet by Bryan Stanley

CHING-A-RING CHAW
(Minstrel Song)

Arranged by AARON COPLAND
Adapted and arranged for clarinet by Bryan Stanley